The *Stornoway Black Pudding* Bible

The marag dubh.

A visit to the Crofter.

The *Stornoway Black Pudding* Bible

Recipes by
Seumas MacInnes

BIRLINN

First published in 2010 by
Birlinn Limited
West Newington House
10 Newington Road
Edinburgh
EH9 1QS

www.birlinn.co.uk

7

ISBN: 978 1 84158 908 4

British Library Cataloguing-in-Publication Data
A catalogue record for this book is available
from the British Library

Designed and typeset by Mark Blackadder

Printed and bound by Bell & Bain Ltd, Glasgow

Contents

Moladh na maraige duibhe

Molt ga mharbhadh
Feòil a' Gheamhraidh
Uain gan reamhrachadh
Am beul na h-oidhch'
Anns an t-sabhal
Seanair le làmh chòir
A' cur às do bheatha
Airson beathachadh àil fhèin

Fuil dhearg ga measgachadh
Le spìosran a' Chinn an Ear
Le geir a' Chinn an Iar
Le min-choirc' chaidh chur le làmh fhèin
Duis ga ghlanadh ri oir a' chladaich

Ga lìonadh le sealbh a shaothair an taic an teine
Ga cheangal le alt an t-seana sheòid
Ga ìoslachadh dhan uisge ghoileach
Plubadaich sa phrais
Blàths is àileadh an teine mònach
An lùib àileadh cùbhraidh na maraige
A' lìonadh chuinnlean nan daoine
Is an aghaidh ri lòn na maidne

Clann bheag le uisg' trom fiaclan
A' cruinneachadh mun bhòrd
Gus an geàrrt' a' mhaodal mhòr.

Is math an còcaire an t-acras!

Foreword

One idle day in 2008, I was browsing the food hall of Harvey Nichols in Edinburgh when a black pudding hit me between the eyes, so to speak. It was the label that startled me, proclaiming the product to be 'Championship-Winning Stornoway-style Black Pudding'. The very small print revealed this object to be the creation of a Portobello butcher.

I experienced two rapid reactions. The first was to recall the maxim about imitation being the sincerest form of flattery – and if 'Stornoway-style Black Pudding' was a sufficiently aspirational piece of branding to find a place in Harvey Nicks, then clearly the genuine article had made a significant impression on the market.

However, my second reaction was to think simply: 'This is a rip-off', and that the people who make the genuine stuff should be helped to do something about it before this ploy went any further. Thus, with the aid of interested local politicians, was born the campaign to have Stornoway black pudding awarded a Protected Designation Order under the European Commission's scheme to defend outstanding regional products against exactly this kind of counterfeiting.

My next stop was Seumas MacInnes at the Café Gandolfi in Glasgow, who had been the first to introduce Stornoway black pudding to chic urban menus. Was there, I wondered, any basis to the imposter's claim to be 'Stornoway-style Black Pudding'? After due tasting, Seumas's majestic reply was: 'There is nothing Stornoway-style about it and in fact, it isn't even a good Lowland black pudding.'

But what is it that makes Stornoway black pudding different and, in the view of ever-growing numbers of connoisseurs, very much better? Seumas's preferred supplier is MacLeod and MacLeod, a third generation family butcher in Stornoway. So who better to ask for the key to the holy grail than Kenny MacLeod, who now presides over that flourishing business? 'All this stuff about secret recipes,' says Kenny. 'It's really very simple . . .' I stop him before he can go further. Nobody wants to hear a magician undermining his own mystique.

What the discussions about Protected Designation status brought to the surface is that Stornoway Black Pudding – the humble *marag dubh* – does now have a real economic significance. Unlike many small towns which have seen the arrival of supermarkets, Stornoway still has a clutch of excellent family butcher shops, each with its own distinctive *marag* output. But according to Kenny, it is now the pudding business that keeps the show on the road, with more than 90 per cent of production going off the island.

His own biggest customer is the MacDonald Hotel chain. Wherever you have breakfast in a MacDonald Hotel – and the group includes such flagship establishments as the Compleat Angler in Marlowe and Edinburgh's Roxburgh Hotel – the certainty is that Stornoway Black Pudding will be on the breakfast menu. This relationship goes back 30 years, when Kenny's father was running the business. Donald MacDonald, a native of Harris, was working for the Reo Stakis Organisation, which started in Glasgow but latterly spread all over the UK. Donald, a man who had known the Stornoway black pudding from birth, introduced the MacLeod and MacLeod product to Stakis hotels. When he started his own MacDonald Hotels group, he naturally retained the same supplier.

But while the MacLeod and MacLeod business had this very substantial foothold in the mainland catering market, it was Seumas MacInnes who took the product into the café and restaurant trade through the legendary Café Gandolfi. Since then, it has been a classic story of how word of mouth – or indeed taste on palate – can be more effective than any other form of advertising. The producers of Stornoway black pudding spend next to nothing on promoting their product but one by one, cafés and restaurants throughout Glasgow, then Scotland, then far beyond, discovered that the magic words 'Stornoway black pudding' created a very effective means of announcing an establishment's commitment to quality Scottish ingredients.

As Kenny MacLeod was about to say before I stopped him, there is nothing fancy about Stornoway black pudding. Its success lies in the fact that it is made to the highest standards, using quality ingredients and without unnecessary embellishments. Kenny points out, for instance, that the interloper in Harvey Nicks contained pork trimmings, which you would never find in genuine Stornoway black pudding. The phrase 'contains meat products', which covers a multitude of sins, is also one to beware of!

It really is the same the whole world over. Black pudding is quintessential peasant food. People were too poor to discard any parts of the animals they bred, so they experimented until they found recipes that created cheap, nourishing and tasty food. There are still croft houses in the Western Isles where home-made *marag dubh* is produced. And that tradition is so recent that no local butcher's version which was not close to the original in quality and purity would have stood a chance. Maybe that is the true key to understanding what makes Stornoway black pudding different, and better.

In Germany, it's Blutwurst, France has boudin noir, Spain and Latin America love their many variations of morcilla, Korea's blood sausage is called soondae . . . In fact, just about every part of the globe has a variation on the same very basic theme. So maybe it is time to internationalise the campaign. We already know that there is nothing in Scotland to compare with Stornoway black pudding and all the wonderful things Seumas can do with it. Tomorrow, the world . . .!

Brian Wilson,
Mangersta, Isle of Lewis
July 2010

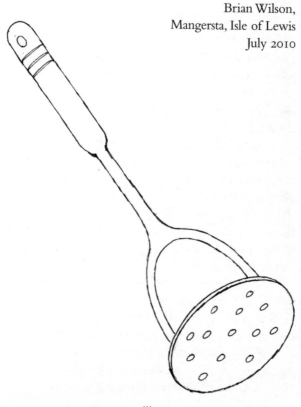

Introduction

The food of the Western Isles never fails to inspire me. The people there have an exceptional passion for good cooking that many others have lost and there is an enviable wealth of superb, fresh ingredients to sustain that enthusiasm.

One of the unique showpieces of that culinary culture – and one of my unchanging favourites – is the *marag dubh*, the black pudding from Stornoway. At Café Gandolfi I think I was the first person in Glasgow to put it on a restaurant menu and it has been a perennial favourite ever since so I think it's appropriate that this books celebrates the myriad uses of this outstandingly good ingredient.

My first memories of *marag dubh* take me back to childhood holidays on Barra, where I was mesmerised by a ritual that was centuries old. First there was the visit to the crofter to collect the stomach and blood of a sheep (no longer possible in these regulated days of course); then the vision of my mother and grandmother on a Hebridean shore washing out the casings in the cold sea;

the vigorous, antiseptic scrubbing of everything in the kitchen and that unforgettable, pungent aroma.

There's a standing joke among my staff that I'm on a ceaseless quest for new recipes that include black pudding and yes, they're probably right. I'm still excited about the many uses for this subtle, spicy food with its distinctive texture, from traditional Scottish recipes through to Spanish dishes and Indian-style food.

My black pudding of choice now comes from Macleod and Macleod of Stornoway, a family butcher who has supplied it to the people of Lewis for almost 80 years. It's not a bad track record: the islanders eat a lot of meat and they have high standards – so if you are cooking with black pudding, buy the very best.

Many of these recipes were revelatory to me and I think will be to others. I've used it in pakoras and dim sum and it's superb in a chorizo and bean stew. You can add it to stews and dumplings, wrap it in pastry and make sausage rolls – or crumble it with carmelised onion and toasted brie.

One of my enduring favourites is Stornoway black pudding with pancakes and mushrooms, fried with onion, garlic, white wine and a dash of sherry vinegar, which teases out a wonderful complexity of flavour.

Stornoway black pudding is a simple, homely food but it has delighted me for years with its distinctive, zesty taste and generous adaptability and I'd be proud to serve it to a discerning clientele anywhere.

Of course, it's still superb with fried eggs and bacon, but I'd like to encourage you to try it in different dishes, to use it in different combinations and to discover it for yourself. How many people actually cook Stornoway black pudding at home? Probably not many – and I hope that this book will change that.

American Sloppy Joes with black pudding

Serves 4

---

1 tablespoon vegetable oil
1 onion, finely chopped
1 red pepper, deseeded and finely chopped
450g minced beef
1 tablespoon plain flour
½ tablespoon thyme
150g black pudding
300ml-can condensed cream of tomato soup
125ml water
½ tablespoon Worcestershire sauce
4 sesame seed rolls
Salt and freshly ground black pepper
Plain crisps to serve

Heat the oil in a large frying pan over a medium heat, add the onion and pepper and cook, stirring frequently for 5–10 minutes until the onion is soft but not brown. Add the minced beef and cook until well browned, stirring constantly with a wooden spoon to break up the meat. Add the crumbled black pudding and continue to cook for 5 minutes.

Sprinkle in the flour and thyme, stirring constantly for a further 2 minutes. Stir in the soup, water and Worcester sauce, and season to taste. Bring to the boil and then simmer for 20 minutes, or until the mince is cooked through.

Put the bottom half of each bun on an individual plate, spoon the sloppy joe mixture onto them and replace the top halves with plain crisps on the side.

Messy, but great.

Aubergine with cinnamon and black pudding

Serves 4

185ml olive oil
1kg aubergine, cut in half lengthwise
3 onions, thinly sliced
3 cloves garlic, finely chopped
400g tomatoes
2 teaspoons oregano
4 tablespoons chopped parsley
35g currents
½ teaspoon ground cinnamon
200g black pudding, chopped
2 tablespoons lemon juice
Pinch of sugar
125ml tomato juice

Pre-heat the oven to 180°C/350°F/gas mark 4.

Heat half the olive oil in a large heavy-based frying pan and cook the aubergine on all sides for 8–10 minutes, until the cut sides are golden. Remove from the pan and scoop out some of the flesh, leaving the skin intact and some flesh lining the skins. Finely chop the scooped-out flesh and set it aside.

Heat the remaining olive oil in the same frying pan and cook the onions until transparent, 10 minutes or so. Add the garlic and then the tomatoes, oregano, parsley, currants, cinnamon, aubergine flesh and black pudding. Place the aubergine shells in an oven-proof dish and fill with the mixture. Mix the lemon juice, sugar and tomato juice together with some seasoning and pour it over the aubergine.

Cover and bake for 30 minutes, then uncover and cook for another 10 minutes before serving.

Black pudding and bacon salad with walnuts and mozzarella

Serves 4

---

2 tablespoons olive oil
250g cubed smoked bacon lardons
100g black pudding
50g walnuts
200g fresh buffalo mozzarella, torn into pieces
100g mixed leaves, rocket is good here
4 tablespoons French dressing
Fresh basil

Heat the oil in a frying pan and begin to cook the bacon. Grill the black pudding on both sides, remove the foil and break into large pieces. Add the walnuts to the bacon and continue until the bacon cubes are crispy.

Divide the salad leaves between 4 plates and do the same with all the other ingredients.

Black pudding and bacon stuffing

Serves 4

Stuffing
3 rashers of smoked bacon, chopped
25g butter
200g black pudding, roughly chopped
1 onion, finely chopped
85g fresh breadcrumbs
2 tablespoons chopped parsley
Finely grated rind of 1 lemon
125 ml dry sherry
1 egg
Salt and freshly ground black pepper

Fry the bacon and the butter, then add the black pudding and the onion and fry until the onion softens and becomes golden. Add the breadcrumbs and cook until they have taken up all the fat and coloured slightly. Add the parsley, lemon rind and sherry and allow to cool. Break the egg into a small bowl and beat well, then add it to the mixture. Season

Stuff into the cavity of a 1.3kg chicken and roast.

Black pudding and rhubarb pastries

Serves 4

---

1 small onion, finely chopped
300g rhubarb, cut into 1cm slices
4 slices of black pudding
2 packets ready-rolled puff pastry cut into 8 15cm squares
150ml cider
Olive oil for frying
Salt and freshly ground black pepper
Pinch or two of grated nutmeg

Preheat oven 180°C/350°F/gas mark 4.

Fry the black pudding in a little olive oil on both sides and then reserve. Add the onion and allow it to soften but not brown, then add the rhubarb and cider and simmer until the rhubarb has formed a sauce. Season and add the nutmeg.

Place the squares of pastry on a lightly floured board and divide the rhubarb among them. Top with half a slice of black pudding. Moisten the edges of the pastry and fold over, pinching the edges together.

With a pastry brush gently brush the pastries with milk and bake for 25–30 minutes, or until golden.

Black pudding croquettes

Serves 4

225g black pudding, peeled and chopped
6 spring onions
1 red pepper, deseeded and chopped
175g mashed potatoes
1 teaspoon Dijon mustard
2 tablespoons red wine vinegar
Salt and freshly ground black pepper
225g fresh breadcrumbs
Oil for frying

Put the spring onion, black pudding and red peppers
into a food processor and process until finely chopped.
Add this to your mashed potato along with the mustard,
vinegar and seasoning, and mix well. Mould the mixture
into cylindrical sausage shapes about 7.5cm long and
2.5cm in diameter. Cool in the fridge and then roll in
the flour, then in the lightly beaten egg and finally in the
breadcrumbs. Heat the oil in a deep frying pan and cook
the croquettes until golden brown on all sides.

Black pudding dumplings for stew

Serves 4

250g self-raising flour
½ teaspoon baking powder
Pinch of salt
1 tablespoon chopped spring onions
60g suet
100g chopped raw black pudding

Sift the flour and baking powder into a bowl. Add the salt and the suet and the other ingredients and mix.

Add enough cold water to form a stiff dough and with two spoons gently lift spoonfuls on to a gently bubbling stew. Continue until you have topped your stew. Cover with a tight-fitting lid and continue cooking for 20 minutes.

Black pudding mash

Serves 4

1.3kg large potatoes
300ml milk
110g spring onions, chopped
110g butter
200g cooked black pudding, chopped

Scrub the potatoes and boil them in their jackets. When cooked, drain and peel. Warm the milk and begin to mash your potatoes with a potato masher or a ricer, or by hand mixer. Add the butter and the rest of the ingredients. Season and serve.

Great with lamb chops or sausages.

Black pudding and
beef Moroccan filo parcels

Serves 4

225g filo pastry sheets
1 egg yolk, beaten
Vegetable oil for frying
Cinnamon for dusting (optional)

The filling
200g crumbled and chopped black pudding
350g lean minced beef
Small onion, finely chopped
1 tablespoon chopped parsley
1 teaspoon cinnamon
Salt and freshly ground black pepper
1 tablespoon olive oil
3 eggs, beaten

Place the oil for the filling in a deep frying pan and then
add all the other filling ingredients and cook for a few
minutes until the moisture evaporates and the meat
separates. Drain off the fat, now add the beaten eggs and
stir in the meat until the eggs are lightly scrambled.
Allow to cool.

Cut the filo sheets into rectangles about 12½cm wide and stack them on top of each other. Take a sheet of pastry and put a heaped teaspoon of filling at one end and fold into a triangle. Stick the loose edge down with a little egg yolk.

Fry in hot oil until crispy and golden. Drain on kitchen paper and serve sprinkled with cinnamon.

Black pudding sausage rolls

Serves 4

---

3 sheets of ready-rolled puff pastry
2 free-range eggs, lightly beaten
600g sausage meat (I usually de-skin good butcher sausages)
200g black pudding, crumbled
2 tablespoons fresh breadcrumbs
3 tablespoons chopped parsley

Pre-heat the oven to 200°C/400°F/gas mark 6, and lightly grease a baking sheet.

Cut the pastry sheets in half and lightly brush the edges with some of the beaten egg. Set aside half of the remaining beaten egg and add the rest to a bowl with all the other ingredients and mix well. Divide the mixture into 6 even portions.

Pipe or spoon the filling down the centre of each piece of pastry, then brush the edges with some of the egg wash. Fold the pastry over the filling, overlapping the edges, and place the join underneath. Brush the rolls with more egg, then cut each into 6 short pieces.

Cut two small slashes on top of each roll, place on the baking trays and bake for 15 minutes.

Reduce the oven temperature to 180°C/350°F/gas mark 4 and bake for another 10–15 minutes or until puffed and golden.

Black pudding skirlie potatoes

Serves 4

1kg floury potatoes
50g butter
1 onion finely chopped
150g medium oatmeal
Salt and freshly ground black pepper
100g black pudding, peeled and finely chopped
2 tablespoons chopped parsley

Boil the potatoes and mash them, but do not add any butter or milk. Melt the butter in a frying pan and gently cook the onion until it begins to brown. Stir in the oatmeal and black pudding, cook for 2–3 minutes, then add the parsley and season. Stir the oatmeal into the mash and shape into small cakes. Brush with a little extra butter and bake in a hot oven for 15 minutes, or until brown and heated through.

Black pudding with mushrooms and pancakes

Serves 8

Black pudding: 2 slices per person
200g button mushrooms
2 cloves garlic
1 onion, finely chopped
Olive oil
White wine
1 tablespoon sherry vinegar
Salt and freshly ground black pepper

Pancakes
200g self- raising flour
2 eggs, beaten
1 dessertspoon syrup
Sugar
140ml milk
50g melted butter

Pre-heat oven to 190°C/375°F/gas mark 5.

First sauté a finely chopped onion in olive oil until transparent. Slice the mushrooms, add them in with the onion and continue to cook for 5–7 minutes. Add half a glass of white wine and the sherry vinegar and cook for a further 5–7 minutes to get all the flavours working together. Season to taste.

For the pancakes, sift the flour with a good pinch of salt. Add the eggs and the rest of the ingredients, beating until a smooth consistency is achieved. Heat a non-stick frying pan over a low to medium heat. Once hot, start to make your pancakes, keeping them fresh and warm in a clean dishtowel.

Cut 2 slices of black pudding per person and cook them in the oven for 10 minutes, turning after 5 minutes.

Broad beans with black pudding on toast

Serves 4

200g black pudding
1 tablespoon olive oil
2 cloves garlic
½ teaspoon fennel seeds
500g fresh broad beans (podded weight)
100ml chicken stock
2 tablespoons chopped fresh mint
Salt and black pepper

Grill the black pudding and then keep it warm. Now add the olive oil to a frying pan along with the garlic and fennel seeds and fry them for a few minutes without letting them colour. Add the broad beans and the stock and simmer until tender. Stir in the mint and season. Add the hot black pudding and serve on toast.

MINT

Cabbage and lamb
with black pudding rolls

Serves 4

---

1 tablespoon olive oil
1 onion, finely chopped
½ teaspoon allspice
1 teaspoon cumin
1 good pinch nutmeg
2 bay leaves
1 large head of cabbage
400g raw minced lamb
150g black pudding
4 cloves garlic, crushed
250g short-grain rice
50g toasted pinenuts
2 tablespoons mint, chopped
2 tablespoons parsley, chopped
1 tablespoon sultanas
250ml olive oil
80ml lemon juice

Heat the oil in a saucepan, add the onion and cook
without colouring for 10 minutes. Add the allspice,
cumin and nutmeg and cook for a further 2 minutes.

Bring a large pot of water to the boil and add the
bay leaves. Cut the tough outer leaves and about 5cm of
the core from the cabbage. Then put the cabbage into
the water and cook for 5 minutes. Carefully loosen a

whole leaf with tongs and remove, continuing until you reach the core. Drain, reserve the liquid and set it aside to cool.

Take 12 leaves of equal size and cut a 'V' from the core of each to remove the thickest part. Trim the central veins so the leaf is as flat as possible. Place two-thirds of the remaining cabbage in the bottom of a very large saucepan.

Now combine the lamb, black pudding, rice, pinenuts, garlic and the onion mixture, mint, parsley and sultanas in a bowl and season well.

With the core end of the leaf closest to you, put 2 tablespoons of the mixture into the centre of the leaf. Roll up, tucking in the sides. Repeat with the remaining leaves and filling. Pack tightly in a single layer over the cabbage in the saucepan and place the remaining third of cabbage on top.

Combine 625ml of the cooking liquor with the olive oil, lemon juice and a teaspoon of salt. Pour this over the cabbage; it should reach the top of the rolls. Bring to the boil then reduce the heat to a gentle simmer and cook for 1¼–1½ hours, then gently remove the rolls and drizzle with some extra olive oil and garnish with a lemon wedge.

Chickpeas with chorizo and black pudding

Serves 4

170g dried chickpeas
1 bay leaf
4 cloves
1 cinnamon stick
750ml chicken stock
2 tablespoons olive oil
1 onion, finely chopped
2 cloves of garlic, crushed
Pinch of thyme
375g chorizo, chopped into dice
200g black pudding
1 tablespoon chopped parsley

Put the chickpeas in a large bowl, cover with water and soak overnight. Drain, then put them in a large saucepan with the bay leaf, cloves, cinnamon and stock. Cover completely with water, bring to the boil, reduce heat and simmer for 1 hour, or until the chickpeas are tender Drain and remove the cloves and cinnamon stick.

Heat the oil in a large frying pan, add the onion and garlic and fry for 10 minutes, until soft and transparent. Add the chorizo and the slices of black pudding and fry for 5 minutes. Add the chickpeas, reduce the heat and continue to cook for an extra 5 minutes. Remove from the heat and add the parsley.

Serve warm or, as in Spain, at room temperature.

Coq au vin
with black pudding

Serves 4

---

2 chickens cut into 8 pieces each
1 bottle full-bodied red wine (burgundy is best)
250g button mushrooms
12 small white onions
3 cloves garlic
2 carrots, peeled and quartered
Vegetable oil
Unsalted butter
1 tablespoon thyme
3 bay leaves
200g black pudding, roughly chopped
1 tablespoon chopped parsley

A day in advance clean and cut your chicken and
marinade it in the red wine, adding the small onions,
carrot and herbs. Cover and put in the fridge.

The next day drain the chicken and vegetables and
keep the marinade.

Brown the chicken and then add the vegetables,
allowing them also to colour. Pour the marinade back
over the chicken and bring to the boil. Add some salt
and pepper and simmer for 1½ hours.

Meanwhile, heat the bacon, garlic and the mushrooms in a skillet for 5 minutes. Add the roughly chopped black pudding and cook for a further 5 minutes.

When the chicken is ready, add the black pudding mixture, season to taste and garnish with chopped parsley.

Creamy celeriac gratin with black pudding

Serves 4

700g potatoes, peeled and thinly sliced
450g celeriac, peeled and thinly sliced
2 bay leaves
20ml milk
200g black pudding, chopped, casing removed
2 cloves garlic, crushed
300ml double cream
25g butter
Salt and freshly ground black pepper

Pre-heat oven to 180°C/350°F/gas mark 4.

Put the potatoes and celeriac into a large saucepan and add the bay leaves and the milk, bring to the boil and then simmer for 5–8 minutes until tender.

Discard the milk and bay leaves. Season the potatoes and celeriac well and put half into a gratin dish. Put the chopped black pudding on top followed by the remaining potato and celeriac. Add the garlic and cream and dot with the butter. Cover with foil and bake for 1 hour.

Remove the foil and allow the top to become golden – should take about 15 minutes. Great on its own, but also as a side with roast chicken.

Cumin and mint hummus with crumbled black pudding and toasted pinenuts

Serves 4

200g chickpeas, soaked with a pinch of bicarbonate of soda
6 tablespoons olive oil
½ large Spanish onion, very finely chopped
½ teaspoon cinnamon
½ teaspoon ground cumin
Juice of 1 lemon
3 cloves garlic, crushed
4 tablespoons tahini paste
150g black pudding
2 tablespoons pinenuts, toasted
Flat-leaf parsley and mint to garnish
Paprika to sprinkle
Sea salt and freshly ground black pepper

Rinse the chickpeas under cold water, then place in a large saucepan. Fill with 2 litres of cold water and bring to the boil then reduce the heat to a gentle simmer, skimming off any scum as it builds up and cook for about 1½–2 hours, or until the skins are tender. Remove from the heat, pour off excess liquid until level with the chickpeas, and season with salt and pepper, then set aside.

Meanwhile heat half the olive oil over a low heat and fry the onion until golden and sweet, then add the cinnamon and cumin.

To make the hummus, drain the chickpeas, keeping aside the cooking liquid, and blend in a food processor with 300ml of cooking liquid. When smooth, add the lemon juice, garlic, tahini and the rest of the olive oil. Season, and add more cooking liquid if necessary.

Spread on to a large serving plate. Now cook the black pudding, remove any casing and sprinkle it over the hummus along with the onion mixture. Top with mint and parsley leaves, paprika and pinenuts.

Great with flatbread or pitta. Just share.

Eggs en cocotte
with black pudding

Serves 4

---

8 free range/organic eggs
150g black pudding, chopped
4 tablespoons double cream
salt and freshly ground black pepper

4 ramekins

Pre-heat oven to 180°C/350°F/gas mark 4.

Divide the black pudding among the ramekins and top with 2 eggs each. Add a tablespoon of cream to each and cook in the oven for 15 minutes. Serve with toast for breakfast or a light salad for lunch.

Eggs Hebridean (Eggs Benedict, but with black pudding)

Serves 4

---

8 very fresh free-range eggs
4 English muffins
4 slices of black pudding

Hollandaise sauce
175g butter
4 egg yolks
1 teaspoon tarragon vinegar

To make the hollandaise sauce, put the butter in a small saucepan and bring to a simmer. Skim off any scum that comes to the surface, then pour the butter into a jug. Put the egg yolks, 2 tablespoons of water and tarragon vinegar into a small food processor or blender, and with the motor running gradually pour in the melted butter. Whizz until creamy and buttery.

Poach your eggs as you would normally, and while doing this cook your black pudding slices in the oven for 10 or 15 minutes. Toast the sliced muffins and arrange them on plates. Remove the black pudding wrapper and divide between the two muffins per portion. Place the poached eggs on top and pour the hollandaise sauce over them. Add freshly ground black pepper and serve.

Eggs, leeks and black pudding Gratin

Serves 4

---

8 free range or organic eggs
4 leeks, cleaned and chopped
100g grated cheddar
1 tablespoon grated parmesan
50g butter
40g plain flour
425ml milk
200g cooked black pudding foil removed and lightly chopped(keep warm)
Salt and freshly ground black pepper

Hard-boil the eggs, peel and keep to the side. Whisk 25g of the butter with the flour into the milk, place on a moderate heat and whisk again until the sauce thickens. Reduce the heat and let it cook for another 5 minutes. Add the parmesan and of the cheddar to the sauce. Now melt the other 25g of butter in a heavy-based saucepan, add the leeks and cook without colouring for 10 minutes.

Place the leeks in the bottom of a 25cm gratin dish that has been lightly buttered, and sprinkle the chopped black pudding over them. Halve the eggs and put them on top of the black pudding, round side up. Check the sauce for seasoning and then pour it over the eggs. Sprinkle the remaining cheddar over the sauce and place the gratin dish under a hot grill to colour. You can warm it all in the oven if you prefer, or think that it needs more of an overall heat.

Fried courgette blossom with ricotta and black pudding

Serves 8

───────────

16–20 courgette blossoms

Filling
350g ricotta
6 tablespoons grated parmesan
1 egg
200g cooked and crumbled black pudding
1 tablespoon chopped parsley
1 tablespoon chopped basil
Salt and freshly ground black pepper

Batter
2 eggs
250g plain flour
Salt and freshly ground black pepper
500ml chilled soda water

Olive oil for frying
Coarse salt to serve

───────────

Soak the courgette blossoms in some cold water to refresh them. Drain carefully and pat dry; as you do this, remove the stamens from inside the flowers.

Mix all the filling ingredients together, taste and season, then place in a piping bag fitted with a plain tip.

Pipe into the blossoms, pinching the tops closed, and set aside.

To make the batter, whisk the eggs until blended, adding the flour, salt and pepper as you whisk. Slowly add the soda water and whisk until smooth; the batter should just coat the back of a wooden spoon.

Pour the oil into a deep sauté pan and allow it to be around 7½cm deep and heat to 180°C/350°F/gas mark 4. Holding a blossom by the stem, dip it into the batter. Let the excess drain away and quickly and gently put it in the oil. Repeat, adding only a few blossoms at a time. Continue to fry them for around 4 minutes, turning them until golden on all sides.

Using a wire skimmer transfer the blossoms to a paper towel to drain briefly. Sprinkle with coarse salt and serve at once.

Halloumi, sundried tomato and black pudding muffins

Makes 12

200g self-raising flour
½ teaspoon baking powder
75g cornmeal
1 teaspoon salt
250g halloumi, grated
10 sundried tomatoes, roughly chopped
150g cooked black pudding, roughly chopped
3 eggs, lightly beaten
300ml milk
4 tablespoons olive oil

Pre-heat oven to 220°C/425°F/gas mark 7.

Line a 12-hole muffin tin with paper casts. Sift the flour, baking powder and salt into a mixing bowl, add the cornmeal. Add the halloumi, sundried tomatoes and black pudding and mix well. Add the remaining ingredients and make sure all is combined together – do not over-mix.

Spoon the mixture into the paper cases and bake for 15–20 minutes. The muffins become golden as they rise.

Hash browns with black pudding and bacon

Serves 4

---

4 plum tomatoes
Sea salt and freshly ground black pepper
8 thin, rindless rashers of bacon
4 slices of black pudding
1 teaspoon honey
6 medium potatoes
1 small onion
1 egg, beaten
1 tablespoon plain flour
2 tablespoons chopped herbs (parsley, chives and chives) CHECK ON PROOF
1 tablespoon olive oil
3 tablespoons vegetable oil

Pre-heat the oven to 200°C/400°F/gas mark 6.

Cut the tomatoes in half lengthwise, season them with salt and pepper and arrange them on a baking sheet. Roll the bacon up and place on the same tray, along with the black pudding. Drizzle the honey over the bacon roll-ups and bake for 15–20 minutes or until the tomatoes are soft and the bacon crisp.

Peel the potatoes and onion, coarsely grate them, then wrap in a clean cloth and squeeze out any excess liquid. Place in a bowl, add the beaten egg, flour, chopped herbs, 1 teaspoon sea salt and the olive oil, and stir well.

Heat 1 tablespoon vegetable oil in a frying pan until hot, then add 2 heaped tablespoons of the potato mixture. Squash them flat and fry gently on both sides until brown. Keep them warm in the oven while you cook the remaining hash browns, adding a little extra oil to the pan each time.

Serve the hash browns topped with the roasted tomato halves, crisp bacon and black pudding.

40

Hebridean boulangerie potatoes

Serves 6

900g potatoes
1 large onion, peeled and sliced into half moons
150ml chicken or vegetable stock
2 thick slices of black pudding

Heat the oven to 180°C/350°F/gas mark 4.

Liberally butter a shallow gratin dish.

Peel and thinly slice the potatoes.

Start with a layer of onions and crumble a slice of the black pudding over them. Repeat the process, building up layer by layer and making sure to finish with a layer of potatoes. Season as you go. Then pour stock over the steak and bake for 1 hour.

Hebridean lamb stew

Serves 4

---

8 small neck fillets of lamb
900g potatoes peeled and sliced
2 large onions
200g black pudding
Salt and freshly ground black pepper
1 tablespoon chopped parsley

Trim some of the fat from the lamb fillets and layer the
potatoes, then the lamb, the black pudding and finally
the onion in an ovenproof dish. Repeat seasoning with
salt and pepper as you go, finishing with a layer of
potatoes. Pour in enough cold water to half-cover the
stew, cover and simmer very gently for 3 hours. Serve
with parsley.

Huevos rancheros with pinto beans and black pudding

Serves 2

---

1 tablespoon olive oil
1 small onion, finely chopped
1 small green pepper, finely chopped
1 red chilli, finely chopped
1 clove garlic, crushed
½ teaspoon dried oregano
1 beef tomato, chopped
400g tin chopped tomatoes
4 free-range eggs
2 flour tortillas
200g tin of pinto beans
150g black pudding, cooked and crumbled

Put the olive oil in a frying pan at a medium heat, add the onions and peppers and fry until soft for 5 minutes. Add the chilli and garlic and stir briefly, then add the oregano, fresh and tinned tomatoes and 90ml water. Bring to the boil and then simmer for 10 minutes. Season with salt and pepper.

Add the pinto beans and the warm black pudding to the tomato sauce and heat through. Smooth the surface of the mixture and make 4 hollows with the back of a wooden spoon or ladle. Break an egg into each hollow, cover the pan with a tight lid and cook for 5 minutes. While the eggs are cooking, warm the flour tortillas.

Sometimes a little feta cheese can be added as a garnish.

Kedgeree with black pudding

Serves 4

450g smoked haddock
1 medium onion, finely chopped
120g butter
2 teaspoons garam masala
1 teaspoon turmeric
350g basmati rice
4 hard-boiled eggs, halved and quartered
300ml double cream, warmed
200g black pudding, cooked and kept warm
Salt and freshly ground black pepper
1 tablespoon chopped parsley

Simmer the haddock in salted water for 15 minutes but be sure not to overcook it.

Drain the fish, keeping the water that it was cooked in. Remove any skin and bones and flake the fish while it is still warm. Fry the onions in the butter along with the turmeric and garam masala until they are soft.

Cook the rice in the haddock water then drain and allow the rice to dry out a little to let the steam dissipate.

Add the fish to the rice with the onions, crumbled black pudding and cream and eggs, sprinkle over the parsley and serve.

Lamb and black pudding burgers with the works

Serves 4

---

2 slices white bread
100ml milk
500g minced lamb
200g chopped black pudding
1 tablespoon chopped parsley
1 tablespoon chopped chives
Sea salt and freshly ground black pepper
1 free range/organic egg
1 tablespoon olive oil

To serve
4 slices blue cheese
4 hamburger rolls
4 tablespoons tomato relish or ketchup
8 lettuce leaves
2 tomatoes, thickly sliced
4 tablespoons mayonnaise

Soak the bread in the milk, squeeze out and chop finely.
In a bowl mix all the burger ingredients together and
when mixed well form into 4 meat patties. Chill until
needed.

Cook the burgers for approximately 5 minutes on
both sides until well browned and cooked through.

Top each burger with the cheese as soon as it comes

off the heat. Split the buns and lightly toast the insides only, top the base bun with, in this order, tomato relish, lettuce leaves, burger and a slice of tomato. Spread the mayonnaise on the inside lid and place on top.

Mushroom and black pudding pakora

Serves 6

110g butter
225g finely chopped onion
450g mushrooms, finely chopped
400g crumbled or processed black pudding
1 tablespoon finely chopped parsley
1 tablespoon finely chopped coriander

The pakora batter
300g gram flour
1 teaspoon chilli powder
1 teaspoon salt
300g natural yoghurt
Juice of 1 lemon

Mix all the batter ingredients together.

Then melt the butter in a heavy-based saucepan on a low heat and add the onions. Allow them to cook gently for 8–10 minutes. Increase the heat and add the mushrooms and cook for 5 minutes. Now fold in the black pudding and the herbs and leave to cool.

Roll the black pudding mixture into balls and dip into the pakora batter.

Cook in hot oil until crisp and golden. Serve with yoghurt or tomato sauce.

Mushrooms stuffed with black pudding

Serves 4

---

4 large or 8 medium-sized field mushrooms
200g black pudding
2 tablespoons chopped parsley
2 tablespoons fresh breadcrumbs

Pre-heat oven to 200°C/400°F/gas mark 6.

Remove and finely chop the mushrooms stems. Wipe the mushroom caps with a damp paper towel to get rid of any grit or dirt, then arrange them gill side upwards into desired dish.

Crumble the black pudding by hand or food processor and add the parsley. Now begin to fill the mushrooms. If you have extra mixture, arrange it around the mushrooms. Sprinkle the breadcrumbs over them and bake for 15–17 minutes.

Serve on their own or with salad as a starter, or for supper between two slices of good bread.

Mutton pasties with black pudding

Serves 8

---

2 breasts of lamb
450g onions peeled
450g potatoes peeled
Salt
Ground black pepper
300g black pudding, chopped and casing removed

For the pastry
450g plain flour
Pinch of salt
350g butter (that you have frozen overnight)
Milk to glaze

Pre-heat oven to 220°C, 425°F, gas mark 7.

Cook the breast of lamb in boiling salted water for about 1½ hours, until tender. Trim away the fat from the breasts and flake the lean meat. Cook the onions and potatoes in the lamb water until tender. Strain and add to the meat along with the chopped black pudding and salt and pepper, mashing the potatoes as you go along.

To make the pastry, sift the flour and salt into a large bowl. Grate the frozen butter into the bowl, pressing with your hands to get the mixture together, then add enough cold water to form a dough that leaves the sides of the bowl clean. Chill for at least 30 minutes before rolling out on a floured surface, then cut it into eight 10–13 cm rounds. Divide the meat into eight and place it in the centre of each round. Dampen the edges of the pastry and draw the edges together to form a seam at the top. Flute the edges with your fingers and brush all over with milk. Cook in the pre-heated oven for 20–25 minutes.

Onions with cheese and black pudding

Serves 4

---

8 medium white onions
2 tablespoons olive oil
200g black pudding, cooked and roughly chopped
4 tablespoons grated parmesan
Pinch of grated nutmeg
Sea salt
Ground black pepper
250ml double cream
Smoked paprika for dusting

Pre-heat the oven to 180°C/350°F/gas mark 4.

Peel the onions and arrange them in a lightly oiled baking tray so that they fit neatly side by side.

Drizzle with the olive oil and bake for 1 hour, or until soft. Now turn up the temperature of the oven to 200°C/390°F/gas mark 6.

Combine the grated cheese, nutmeg, sea salt, black pepper and cream in a jug and mix well. Place the chopped black pudding over the onions and pour the cream over that. Return to the oven and bake for a further 10 minutes, sprinkle with the smoked paprika and serve with a salad or as a side dish for roast lamb.

Paella of monkfish and black pudding

Serves 4

---

8 tablespoons olive oil
400g monkfish, trimmed and cut into 3cm pieces
2 large onions, finely chopped
2 green peppers, deseeded and finely chopped
6 cloves garlic, finely chopped
½ teaspoon fennel seeds
800ml fish stock, heated
½ teaspoon saffron threads
250g paella rice
80ml white wine
2 tablespoons chopped parsley
200g black pudding, peeled, cooked and chopped
1 teaspoon smoked paprika
250g piquillo peppers, roughly chopped
Seasoning

Heat 3 tablespoons of the olive oil in a paella pan or
deep frying pan over a medium heat. Carefully add the
monkfish to the pan and stir-fry until almost cooked.
Remove from the pan and set aside in a bowl.

Add the remaining oil to the cleaned pan, then add
the onions and peppers and cook on a medium heat for
20 minutes, stirring from time to time.

Turn the heat down and add the garlic and fennel seeds and cook for 10 minutes. As this is being done add the saffron to the hot fish stock and let it infuse for 10 minutes.

Put the rice into the onions and mix.

Turn the heat up on the paella pan and add the wine followed by the hot stock. Add the paprika and some seasoning. Simmer for 10 minutes and top with the monkfish and its juices and try and let the stock top the fish, by pushing it down into the pan. Keep moving the pan to stop things sticking, and also try to stop yourself from stirring it. Cook for 5 minutes more, then add the black pudding with the parsley and take the paella off the heat and cover it. Let it rest for 5 minutes, remove the lid and garnish with wedges of lemon and chopped red peppers.

Pissaladière with black pudding and anchovies

Serves 6

Dough
2 teaspoons dried yeast
250g plain flour
60ml olive oil

Topping
40g butter
2 tablespoons olive oil
1.5kg onions, thinly sliced
2 tablespoons thyme
Extra olive oil for brushing
200g crumbled black pudding
16 anchovies, halved lengthwise
24 pitted black olives

Mix the yeast with 125ml warm water. Leave in a draught-free place for 10 minutes or until bubbles appear on the surface. Sift the flour into a large bowl, add half a teaspoon of salt, the olive oil and the yeast mixture. Mix until the dough clumps together and forms a ball. Turn out onto a lightly floured work surface and knead the dough, adding a little more flour or a few drops of warm water if necessary until you have a soft dough that is not sticky but dry to the touch.

Knead for 10 minutes or until smooth and the impression made by a finger springs back immediately.

Rub the inside of a bowl with olive oil. Roll the ball of dough around in the bowl to coat it with oil, then cut a shallow cross on the top of the ball with a knife. Place the dough in the bowl, cover with clingfilm and leave in a draught-free place for 1–1½ hours, or until the dough has doubled in size. Gently knock back the dough by punching it with your fist and then knead it again for a couple of minutes. Leave in a draught-free place to rise until doubled in size.

Melt the butter with the olive oil in a saucepan and add the onion and half the thyme. Cover and cook for 1 hour on a low heat, stirring from time to time, until the onions are soft but not brown, cool and then add the crumbled black pudding.

Meanwhile pre-heat oven to 200°C/400°F/gas mark 6.

Roll the dough to roughly fill a greased 34 × 36cm shallow baking tray. Brush the dough with the olive oil, then spread the onion and black pudding over it.

Lay the anchovies in a lattice pattern over the onions and arrange the olives in the lattice diamonds. Bake for 20 minutes or until the dough is cooked and lightly browned. Sprinkle with the remaining thyme and serve.

Potato scones with black pudding

Makes 15–20

225g cooked potato
50g plain flour
75g cooked and chopped black pudding
Pinch of salt

Mash the potatoes until smooth, then gently work in as much flour as they will absorb. Roll out the dough as thinly as you can and sprinkle the black pudding over it. Fold over the dough and roll it out as thinly as you can again. Cut it into rounds, place it on a hot griddle and prick them a few times with a fork, then cook for 2–3 minutes on either side. Cool the scones between a folded tea-towel before serving.

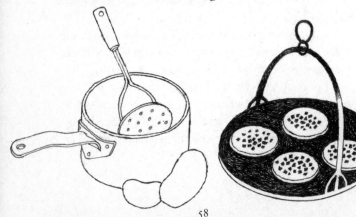

Potatoes with mustard seeds and crumbled black pudding

Serves 4

450g large new potatoes, scrubbed
Sea salt
½ tablespoon vegetable oil
1 medium onion, finely chopped
1 clove garlic, crushed
½ teaspoon Dijon mustard
2 tablespoons brown mustard seeds
200g chopped black pudding
2 tablespoons chopped parsley

Boil the potatoes in salted water until tender, then drain and slice thickly.

Heat the oil in a large pan, and fry the onion until soft and golden. Add the garlic and the mustard and cook for 2–5 minutes, then add the mustard seeds and when they begin to pop add the potatoes and the black pudding. Stir gently for 10 minutes. Keeping the potatoes whole, allow them to colour slightly as the black pudding cooks.

Serve garnished with the fresh parsley.

Rabbit casserole with mustard, wine and black pudding sauce

Serves 4

2 tablespoons olive oil
1.5kg rabbit pieces
2 onions, sliced
85g cubed bacon lardons
2 tablespoons plain flour
375ml chicken stock
175ml dry white wine
1 teaspoon fresh thyme
200g crumbled black pudding
125ml double cream
2 tablespoons Dijon mustard

Pre-heat the oven 180°C/350°F/gas mark 4.

Heat half the oil in the casserole dish and brown the
rabbit in batches adding more oil when needed.
Remove the rabbit and add the onion and bacon to the
dish and cook, stirring all the time for 5 minutes.
Sprinkle in the flour and with a wooden spoon scrape
all the residue from the bottom. Add the stock and wine
and stir until the sauce has come to the boil. Return the
rabbit to the dish and continue to cook in the oven for
1 hour. Then stir in the black pudding and cook for a
further 30 minutes. The rabbit should be tender now so
add the cream and mustard, check for seasoning and if
you have more fresh thyme, add it now!

Ricotta, tomato and black pudding quiche

Serves 4

Packet ready-made short-cut pastry
200g ricotta cheese
200g black pudding – cooked grilled on both sides
4 spring onions, chopped and cooked FRIED?
10 cherry tomatoes, halved
250ml double cream
3 eggs lightly beaten
Salt and freshly ground black pepper

Pre-heat oven to 200°C/400°F/gas mark 6.

Line a 25cm fluted loose-based tin with ready-made short-crust pastry.

Blind-bake the pastry case for 10 minutes.

Whisk together the eggs and cream and season with a little salt and freshly ground black pepper.

Reduce the oven to 180°C/350°F/gas mark 4.

Crumble the cheese on top of the pastry along with the black pudding and spring onions. Now add the cherry tomatoes. Pour the egg and cream custard over it all and bake for 30 minutes.

Roasted asparagus with black pudding

Serves 4

---

2 large bunches asparagus
200g black pudding
1 tablespoon olive oil

Pre-heat oven to 180°C/350°F/gas mark 4.

Place asparagus on a baking sheet, drizzle the tips with the olive oil and then crumble the black pudding onto the rest of the asparagus. Bake for 15 minutes or until the vegetables are cooked.

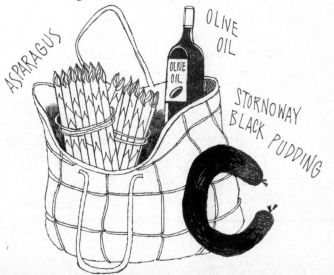

Salt cod and black pudding fritters

Serves 4

500g salt cod
1 large potato, unpeeled
2 tablespoons milk
60ml olive oil
1 small onion, finely chopped
2 cloves garlic, crushed
100g black pudding, chopped
30g self-raising flour
2 eggs, separated
1 tablespoon chopped parsley
Oil for frying

Soak the cod in cold water for 24–48 hours, changing the water regularly to remove as much salt as possible.

Cook the potato in boiling water until done, then mash with the milk and 2 tablespoons of olive oil.

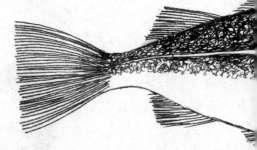

Drain the cod, cut it into large pieces and place it in a saucepan. Cover with water and bring it to the boil, allow it to simmer for 15 minutes and then drain. When it is cool enough to handle, remove the skin and any bones, then mash well with a fork until flaky.

Heat the remaining olive oil in a frying pan and cook the onion for about 10 minutes over a medium heat until tender. Add the garlic and black pudding and cook for 5 minutes.

Combine the cod, potato, onion, flour, egg yolks and parsley in a bowl and season. Whisk the egg whites until stiff, then fold them into the mixture.

Deep-fry the mixture in hot oil by dropping in a tablespoon at a time, cook for 2 minutes or until golden and puffed. Drain on kitchen paper and serve.

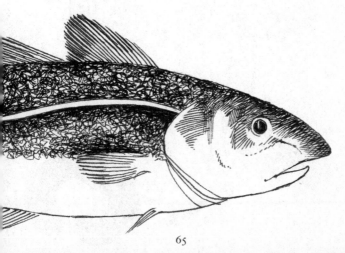

Scones with caramelised onion and black pudding

Makes 16–18 scones

350g self-raising flour
½ teaspoon baking powder
Pinch of salt
150g black pudding, cooked and roughly chopped
1 onion, finely chopped
1 tablespoon oil
50g butter
1 egg
Milk to mix

Pre-heat oven to 230°C/450°F/gas mark 8.

Start by frying the onions in the vegetable oil and allowing them to become lightly coloured and sweet, around 15–20 minutes.

Sift the flour, baking powder and salt into a bowl, rub in the butter to make it resemble breadcrumbs, add the black pudding and the cooled onions (drained as much as possible of the oil). Add the egg and enough milk to make a soft dough. Knead on a formed board to 1½cm thick and cut into circles using a scone cutter.

Bake for 8–10 minutes.

Great with soup, on their own or even topped with garlic prawns.

Spiced bean and black pudding stew

Serves a hungry 4

---

3 tablespoons olive oil
2 onions, chopped
3 cloves garlic, crushed
1 tablespoon paprika
1 red chilli, deseeded and chopped
700g sweet potatoes, peeled and cubed
700g pumpkin, peeled and cubed
125g okra
500g passata
200g black pudding, grilled on both sides and kept warm
400g can cannelloni beans, drained

Heat the oil in a large, heavy-based saucepan, add the onions and garlic and allow to cook for 10 minutes. Stir in the paprika and chilli and cook for 2 minutes before adding the sweet potatoes, pumpkin, okra, passata and 900ml water. Season well with salt and pepper. Cover and simmer for 20 minutes.

Now add the beans and mix before placing the black pudding on top. Cook for 5 minutes to warm the beans. Great with some good bread and a salad.

Spicy corn bread with chilli black pudding and goat's cheese

Serves 8

350g cornmeal
375g plain flour
150g sugar
½ teaspoon salt
½ tablespoon baking powder
8 tablespoons melted butter
350ml buttermilk
100ml milk
2 beaten eggs
1 teaspoon Tabasco
100ml tinned corn kernels
75g crumbled goat's cheese
60g spring onion, finely chopped
100g black pudding, cooked and crumbled
2 tablespoons coriander, chopped

Pre-heat oven to 220°C/425°F/gas mark 7.

Put the first five ingredients into a large bowl. In another bowl mix all the remaining ingredients and then add them to the first bowl.

Pour the mixture into a large roasting tray; the mixture should come about two-thirds of the way up the side of the tin. Bake for 20–25 minutes until golden and a skewer comes out clean.

Eat while warm with . . .

Stir-fried cabbage with black pudding topping

Serves 4 to 6

---

1 Savoy cabbage, shredded
2 tablespoons vegetable oil
2 cloves garlic
100g cooked and crumbled black pudding, kept hot

Heat wok and add oil, quickly add the cabbage and garlic and stir for 3–5 minutes until cooked. Put into a warm serving dish and sprinkle the hot black pudding over.

Stolen chicken with black pudding

Serves 4

---

12 chicken thighs, skin on
20 small new potatoes, skin on
1 lemon, juiced and peeled
4 cloves garlic, peeled and crushed
6 tablespoons olive oil
Salt and freshly ground black pepper
200g black pudding, peeled and cut into quarters
1 tablespoon chopped parsley

Pre-heat oven to 180°C/350°F/gas mark 4.

Slash the chicken thighs 2 or 3 times and put them into a large bowl with the potatoes.

Mix together the lemon juice, the olive oil and the crushed garlic and pour them over the chicken and potatoes. Put the chicken and potatoes in a single layer in a large roasting pan, season well with salt and pepper and add the lemon skin into the roasting pan.

Roast in the oven for 30 minutes, then add the black pudding and continue to cook for a further 15 minutes. Sprinkle with the chopped parsley and serve.

Toad in the hole with black pudding

Serves 4

---

6 large sausages
4 thick slices (350g) black puddingg cut into semi-circles, with any
foil removed
1 tablespoon vegetable oil

Batter
110g plain flour
2 eggs
300ml milk
Salt and freshly ground black pepper

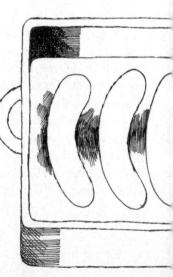

Pre-heat oven to 220°C/425°F/gas mark 7.

Bake the sausages for 5 minutes then add the black pudding and continue for another 5 minutes, turning once to colour the other side.

Make the batter by sifting the flour into a mixing bowl and then add the eggs and milk and whisk until a smooth batter is achieved.

Pour the batter over the sausages and black pudding and bake for a further 40-45 minutes or until the batter is risen and golden.

Serve immediately with a salad or just some brown sauce.

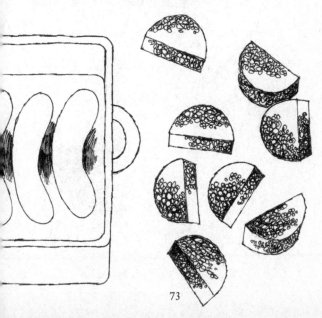

Tortilla with black pudding

Serves 6

500g potatoes, peeled and cut into 1cm slices
60ml olive oil
1 large onion, thinly sliced
4 cloves garlic
150g black pudding, peeled and chopped
2 tablespoons finely chopped parsley
6 free range/organic eggs

Put the potato slices in a large saucepan, cover with cold water and bring to the boil, continue to cook for 5 minutes, drain and set aside.

Put the oil in a deep-sided non-stick frying pan and add the onions, allow them to cook on a medium heat for 20 minutes, then add the garlic and cook for a further 10 minutes. Add the potatoes, black pudding and parsley, stir to combine and cook for 5 minutes. Whisk the eggs with a teaspoon of salt and some black pepper and pour them over the potatoes. Cover and cook for 20 minutes over a low to medium heat. If the top is still runny, finish it off under the grill. Slide off onto a shiny dish and eat hot or cold. Great for a picnic.

Venison casserole with black pudding

Serves 4

---

2 rosemary sprigs, leaves removed and chopped
2 onions, chopped
2 cloves garlic
85g prosciutto, chopped
100g butter
1kg venison, cut into large cubes
1 litre good beef stock
200ml robust red wine
75ml red wine vinegar
4 cloves
4 juniper berries, crushed
2 bay leaves
3 tablespoons plain flour
125ml marsala
2 teaspoons lemon zest
2 tablespoons chopped parsley
200g cooked black pudding, chopped

Heat half the butter in a large heavy-based
saucepan, add the chopped onion, rosemary,
garlic and prosciutto and soften at a low heat. Add the
venison and cook for a further 10 minutes, browning
on all sides. Add the vinegar and red wine and allow
to reduce by half. Add half of the beef stock with the
cloves, crushed juniper berries and bay leaf. Allow to
simmer for around 1 hour.

Meanwhile, melt the remaining butter, stir in the flour and cook at a moderate heat for 5 minutes. Slowly add the remaining stock and cook until it thickens. Stir into the venison with the marsala and black pudding, then cook for 30 minutes or until tender. Check seasoning and garnish with the parsley and lemon zest.

Warm salad of scallops, black pudding and pea and mint purée

Serves 4

2 tablespoons vegetable oil
4 slices of black pudding, each approx. 1cm thick
12 large Scottish scallops
Salt and freshly ground black pepper

Pea and mint purée
55g unsalted butter
6 spring onions, finely sliced
60g frozen peas
1 teaspoon sugar
½ pint vegetable stock
2 tablespoons of fresh mint, roughly chopped
150ml of double cream

For the purée, add the butter to a medium-sized saucepan, and as it starts to foam add the spring onions and allow them to soften. Add the peas and sugar and stir, reduce the heat and put a tight-fitting lid on the pan and stew for 5–7 minutes. Take the lid off and allow the liquid to reduce. Add the cream and mint and continue until it thickens. Transfer to a food processor and blend until smooth but still with texture, and then season.

Grill the black pudding on both sides and keep warm.

Season the scallops and place them on a lightly greased, but very hot, frying pan and stir for 1 minute on both sides.

Arrange the black pudding in the centre of your plate and top with the scallops. Dot the pea and mint purée around the dish and garnish with more fresh mint. Serve with lemon or even a splash of sherry vinegar.

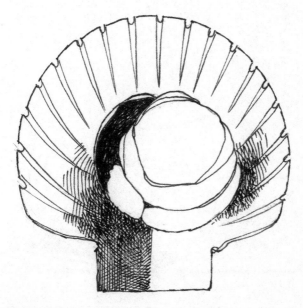